**A 40 Day Devotional
and Small Group Study**

CRAIG MATTES

A FiveTwo Network publication

MEET JESUS

A 40 Day Devotional and Small Group Study

CRAIG MATTES

A FiveTwo Network publication

Meet Jesus

40 Day Devotional and Small Group Study.

© Copyright 2015 by Craig Mattes. All rights reserved.

No part of this book may be reproduced in any written, electronic, recording, or photocopying without written permission of the publisher or author. The exception would be in the case of brief quotations embodied in the critical articles and reviews and pages where permission is specifically granted by the publisher or author.

Scripture quotations are from The Holy Bible, English Standard Version (ESV), copyright 2001 by Crossway, a publishing ministry of Good News Publishers. Used by permission. All rights reserved.

Scripture quotations marked (NLT) are taken from the Holy Bible, New Living Translation, copyright © 1996, 2004, 2007 by Tyndale House Foundation. Used by permission of Tyndale House Publishers, Inc., Carol Stream, Illinois 60188. All rights reserved.

Scripture taken from The Message. Copyright © 1993, 1994, 1995, 1996, 2000, 2001, 2002. Used by permission of NavPress Publishing Group.

Also used - THE HOLY BIBLE, NEW INTERNATIONAL VERSION®, NIV® Copyright © 1973, 1978, 1984, 2011 by Biblica, Inc.® Used by permission. All rights reserved worldwide.

Additional copies may be purchased by contacting:
FiveTwo
PO Box 6526
Katy, TX 77491

fivetwo.com

let's start something new.

We exist to fuel a movement
of Christian startups that
help grow Jesus' Church.

Discover camaraderie and
accountability in a Local.

Receive the know-how and support
to launch a sustainable startup
in our StartNew incubator.

Get connected with other Christian
entrepreneurs at an O2 event.

fivetwo.com

FOREWORD

Talking about Jesus flows comfortably from someone who knows Jesus. Knows as in really knows. As in you have talked with Him, sought His advice, and followed His counsel.

As the biblical illiteracy rate increases in the Western Church, we need a focused approach to help people meet again the Person around whom all persons revolve. We need a primer, you might say, that introduces us to the Source of all we see and the hope which we all seek.

I spend the majority of my time working with entrepreneurial leaders who want Jesus to be obvious in their vocation, especially in the startups they launch. And yet how does that happen without creating a sub-culture or time warp? Are there best practices that can be employed so that the faith that lives inside lives also outside, especially through words?

We published this work as a way for people to not only meet the divinely multi-faceted Jesus but to also be confident and eloquent in how they talk about Him with the people in their lives. Whether you call them hats or roles, titles or attributes,

Craig creates devotional moments that both expand and deepen our knowledge of Jesus and His life. All so that we can readily speak Him into the lives of those we meet.

I hope this work deepens your love, knowledge and trust in Jesus so that you more actively speak of Him with others.

Peace,

Bill Woolsey
Executive Director, FiveTwo Network

IN MEMORY

of my dad, William Mattes, who is now meeting with
our Lord and Savior Jesus in heaven.
Thanks, Dad (and Mom too of course),
for introducing me to Jesus!

INTRODUCTION

The meaning around **MEET JESUS** is two-fold. The first meaning reflects us introducing people to Jesus. Each day's devotion will help the reader discover a different characteristic/identity of Jesus (Savior, Redeemer, Prince of Peace, etc.). As we go about our lives making disciples, telling people of Jesus, it is helpful to offer some more specific introductions as to who Jesus is. So as we would introduce two friends who don't know each other to one another, we would introduce our friends and those we encounter, as we go about our lives, to our friend, Jesus.

The second meaning simply reminds us of the importance of meeting *with* Jesus. As we are in the Word learning new aspects on who Jesus is, we will do this all with Him. In that time with Him we will be spiritually renewed, refreshed, and reminded that "It's in Christ that we find out who we are and what we are living for." (Ephesians 1:11a MSG)

DAY 1
MEET JESUS
ADVOCATE
1 JOHN 2:1

"My dear children, I am writing this to you so that you will not sin. But if anyone does sin, we have an advocate who pleads our case before the Father. He is Jesus Christ, the one who is truly righteous. He himself is the sacrifice that atones for our sins—and not only our sins but the sins of all the world." (1 John 2:1-2 NLT)

How would you define the word *advocate*?

What does *Jesus: Advocate* mean to you?

What would *Jesus: Advocate* mean to one who does not-yet-know Him?

Read Luke 4:38-41.

A couple things we know from this passage on *Jesus: Healer*:

1. He heard the requests from others to heal.

2. Jesus has the power to heal anything - "No matter what their diseases were, the touch of his hand healed everyone."

What else about *Jesus: Healer* do you find in Luke 4:38-41?

How have you witnessed Jesus' healing hand—in your life or in the life of another?

How does what you know of *Jesus: Healer* inform and impact your day with those you encounter (those in need of healing...whether physically, emotionally, or spiritually)?

Read John 6:22-59.

"...don't be so concerned about perishable things like food. Spend your energy seeking the eternal life that the Son of Man can give you." (John 6:27 NLT)

What other perishable things do we often concern ourselves with and expend much energy towards? What is it that makes these things so perishable?

"I am the bread of life. Whoever comes to me will never be hungry again. Whoever believes in me will never be thirsty." (John 6:35 NLT).

"I tell you the truth, anyone who believes has eternal life. Yes, I am the bread of life! Your ancestors ate manna in the wilderness, but they all died. Anyone who eats the bread from heaven, however, will never die. I am the living bread that came down from heaven. Anyone who eats this bread will live forever; and this bread, which I will offer so the world may live, is my flesh." (John 6:47-51 NLT)

Jesus: Bread of Life is anything but perishable. He is everlasting. In Him we have fullness, complete satisfaction. God sent bread from heaven (manna) to nourish the Israelites' 40 year journey in the wilderness. Then to ultimately satisfy the souls of His people, God sent Himself, Jesus Christ, the Bread of Life, so that we would live forever.

What does/could it mean to meet *Jesus: Bread of Life*? What is the risk/reward for seeking not the perishable but the eternal?

Who do you know in need of this bread of life? How may you introduce this person to Jesus?

Read Luke 4:42-44.

"I [Jesus] must preach the Good News of the Kingdom of God in other towns, too, because that is why I was sent." (Luke 4:43 NLT)

Jesus was a man on mission to bring the Good News of the Kingdom of God to the world. In fact, He brought Himself. He is the mission!

Carl Medearis in his book *Speaking of Jesus* put it so well, "Jesus didn't come to build a kingdom. He brought one with Him. He is the kingdom. He is the entry point...Wherever He went, the pained and lost people He met followed Him. Jesus' gospel was that He was the kingdom of heaven, with an easy and light yoke. He was available, and He was compassionate. And it appears that He was making house calls."

Younger readers may be asking, "What's a house call?" Back in the day doctors would come right to the house of those who are sick. Now we need to go to their offices.

We, the sinful, the sick, the lost, in need of a Savior, a Healer, can be thankful that we don't need to go to God. His Kingdom, His "office", He Himself, carrying the power of healing and forgiveness, came to us!

What does this mean to you?

If you are a follower of Jesus, you follow what He is about. This is what He is about. This is why He was sent. What is then *our* mission? How are you about Jesus' mission? How do we introduce *Jesus: Man on Mission* with others?

Read John 1:3-4.

"God created everything through him, and nothing was created except through him. The Word gave life to everything that was created, and his life brought light to everyone." (John 1:3-4 NLT)

I love being out in nature. Whether it is hiking a dirt path or running a crushed gravel trail, I soak all of creation in—the sights, the sounds and the smells. It is during these moments when I feel I'm in my best posture to think of and pray to *Jesus: Creator*.

"You are worthy, O Lord our God, to receive glory and honor and power. For you created all things, and they exist because you created what you pleased." (Revelation 4:11 NLT)

Next time you are out on the trails or simply looking out your window, ponder the complexity of creation. An accident. I think not. To hold all in balance, how can there not be a Creator who put all of this universe into motion? And who does Scripture say brought life to the world - the Word, Jesus.

What thoughts run through your mind when seeing/sensing the evidence of *Jesus: Creator*?

When sharing Jesus, maybe this is one of the easiest, most tangible aspects of Jesus' identity to introduce one to. How may you introduce Jesus to another in such a way today, this week?

Read Luke 5:1-11.

How do you see Jesus impacting people's lives in this passage?

In these verses I see it happening both on the macro and the micro level.

"...great crowds pressed in on him to listen to the word of God." (Luke 5:1b NLT)

On the macro level here is Jesus and a great crowd. Picture the scene.

People pressing in on one another to hear Jesus preach and teach the word of God. I imagine one couldn't get close enough to hear the words dripping from His lips. These couldn't have been words that made little impact on people's lives, otherwise they wouldn't be there. These were life changing and life giving words.

Then on the micro level is Jesus and Simon.

"When he had finished speaking, he said to Simon, 'Now go out where it is deeper, and let down your nets to catch some fish.' 'Master,' Simon replied, 'we worked hard all last night and didn't catch a thing. But if you say so, I'll let the nets down again.' And this time their nets were so full of fish they began to tear!" (Luke 5:4-6 NLT)

Peter's initial reply carried a hint of reluctance. I imagine a pause between sentences. Peter continued, "But if you say so..."

Then look at the life impact, the life change.

"[Jesus replied] 'From now on you'll be fishing for people!'
And as soon as they landed, they left everything and followed Jesus."
(Luke 5:10 NLT)

No reluctance. Leaving everything. Following Jesus.

How has Jesus impacted you, changed the direction of your life? To whom might you share that story? And know that as you share that story (your story of faith), you introduce *Jesus: Life Impacter* to another.

Jesus said, "Yes, I am the gate. Those who come in through me will be saved. They will come and go freely and will find good pastures." (John 10:9 NLT)

Jesus later explained, "I am the way, the truth, and the life. No one can come to the Father except through me."

People of different world faiths say that there are all sorts of ways to God, to heaven—all of which involve man doing something to earn that entrance. You can say that such religions have an entrance fee to heaven. You need to give something to whoever/whatever is working the front gate.

Disney World offers a FastPass system to allow ticketholders shorter lines to the most popular rides and attractions. You receive your FastPass passes after you've paid your expensive ticket price.

Imagine with Jesus (and I know this is a stretch), that as you come to the Gate—Himself—you are given a FastPass to God immediately. Your entrance, in fact, is free because He, Jesus, has paid the price of your admission. This was done by His work on the cross, dying for your sins.

This is just one way of explaining *Jesus: Gate* to another. How else might you make this introduction?

Worship   **5 minutes**

To whomever is the Worship leader: Choose a hymn/song that touches you as to who Jesus is. Play the song for the group. Share how you personally **MEET JESUS** through this song. Be sure to take turns with this each week.

Devotional Discussion   **45 minutes**

OPTION 1
Discuss, in order, the questions presented in Day 1 thru 7's devotions.
OPTION 2
Discuss which reading from Day 1 thru 7 spiritually challenged you the most? Why was that? What next step is Jesus calling you to take?

Helping Others MEET JESUS   **15 minutes**

        Jesus stated, "As you sent me into the world,
    so I have sent them into the world." (John 17:18 ESV)

       James stated, "Do not merely listen to the word,
and so deceive yourselves. Do what it says." (James 1:22 NLT)

What can your group do to put these verses into practice?
Over the next several weeks, your small group will select, plan, and initiate an effort to impact the community so that they may **MEET JESUS**. This effort would ideally happen before session 6's small group meeting. The nature and scope of this is up to you. It could be volunteering at a homeless shelter. It could be buying coffee for patrons at a local coffee shop with no strings attached. It could be planning an event that would bless your next door neighbors. The ideas are endless.

If someone has an idea right now to share, feel free. Otherwise, wait to talk through this in more detail next week after group members have had time to think/pray about it.

Prayer   **20 minutes**

Share a prayer request based on what was discussed during this meeting's Devotional Discussion and/or Helping Others **MEET JESUS** time. What is that next step in your faith life God is calling you to make? What convicted you from God's Word and/or our discussion of His Word? Please also share a way in which the group may support/encourage you regarding what you've shared. Of course other important matters can be prayed about as well. After all have shared, pray for the person on your left (whether aloud or silently). Pray together in popcorn style (as opposed to going in order around a circle).

Coordinating next week's meeting   **5 minutes**

Study Components	Study Component Leader
Worship	
Devotional Discussion	
Helping Others Meet Jesus	
Prayer	
Coordinating	

<u>***Worship Leader***</u>
Leads worship time during meeting.
<u>***Devotional Discussion Leader***</u>
Leads the Bible Study time, encourages application of God's Word to life.
<u>***Helping Others MEET JESUS Leader***</u>
Leads the effort to impact the community to **MEET JESUS**.
<u>***Prayer Leader***</u>
Leads the group prayer time.
<u>***Coordinating Leader***</u>
Coordinates and reminds who will lead the different meeting components..

Read Luke 5:12-16.

As miraculous as Jesus' act of healing was for the man with leprosy, as I read this text the phrase that most caught my attention was "Jesus reached out and touched him." (Luke 5:13a NLT)

Jesus didn't need to touch the man to heal him. Look at Jesus' power in healing the young servant of Cornelius in Matthew 8:5-13. But you can say that reaching down and reaching out in forms of physical care was (and continues to be...more on this below) Jesus' modus operandi.

To be honest, I was trying to find a better word than compassionate. It is the first word I thought of, but it almost seems like a word we toss around a lot and sounds similar to sympathy. Not to give sympathy a negative context, but one does not need to physically connect with a person to sympathize. He or she can do it from a distance, whether the person to whom sympathy is extended to knows it or not.

But when you break it down, *compassionate* or *compassion* is exactly the right word here. *Com* meaning with (think of *communion* -people coming together). *Passion* stemming from *pati* meaning *to suffer*.

Compassionate - one who suffers with another. That is Jesus.

So we have Jesus in this account not just looking from a distance at this highly contagious and fatally ill person, but comes forward, reaches out and touches the person. Imagine how many people had reached out to touch this man since he was afflicted. I'm guessing the count was zero.

Yet no matter our affliction, addiction, sin, whatever we find debilitating and out-casting from others, Jesus comes to us. Some of the tangible ways He comes to us are through the Sacraments of Baptism and the Lord's Supper. These are physical means Jesus works through in demonstrating His compassion and grace to us today and now. He also uses His followers, as they carry the Good News found in His Word, to extend His compassion and care.

What else of Jesus' compassion strikes you in this account?

In the past, how have you demonstrated Jesus' compassion to another? How is God "messing" with you these days in showing His compassion, introducing *Jesus: Compassionate*, with one who is suffering—maybe in a situation you find yourself resisting?

What are some reasons we resist or withhold compassion? What are the risks involved?

How is Jesus calling you to grow with compassion, namely His compassion?

DAY 9
MEET JESUS
GOOD SHEPHERD
JOHN 10:11, 14-16

Jesus said, "I am the good shepherd. The good shepherd sacrifices his life for the sheep. I am the good shepherd; I know my own sheep, and they know me, just as my Father knows me and I know the Father. So I sacrifice my life for the sheep." (Luke 10:11, 14-15 NLT)

What kind of shepherd is Jesus? Well,
1) He is good. What makes him good?
2) Jesus sacrificed Himself on the cross for His sheep.

Sheep are not the smartest of animals. Similarly, man, since Adam, has made many poor choices, sinful ones, decisions which rebelled against God's ways. But despite His sheep straying from the path, He sent His Son, our Good Shepherd, to bring us back into the fold with God, our Father. *Jesus: Good Shepherd* went to whatever lengths so that His sheep would not perish but have eternal life with God. *Jesus: Good Shepherd* sacrificed Himself on the cross, paying the penalty for our sheepish, shameful, sinful decisions.

And *Jesus: Good Shepherd's* work is not yet done
(and we have a role in this):

"I have other sheep, too, that are not in this sheepfold. I must bring them also. They will listen to my voice, and there will be one flock with one shepherd." (John 10:14-16 NLT)

There are more sheep out there yet to be brought into the fold. (Read also Jesus' parable of the lost sheep.) There are more to reach and save with Jesus' love. There are more to tell of *Jesus: Good Shepherd's* sacrifice. We have this in our hands, the Word, His words as found in the Bible.

What are different ways we may introduce *Jesus: Good Shepherd* so that others would listen to His voice and come to Him?

Read Luke 5:17-26.

Not to downplay at all the miracle of healing Jesus performed on the young paralytic man, but the truly outstanding work of Jesus done by Him in this account was His forgiveness of sin. "Young man, your sins are forgiven." (Luke 5:20b NLT) Jesus had the power to forgive one's lifetime accumulation of sins (countless as they were), rebellions, addictions, stupid decisions, self-centered motives, etc.

The Pharisee were aghast, "Only God can forgive sins!" (Luke 5:21b NLT)

Yep. That is who forgave them. And Jesus has the power to continue forgiving sin. He has the power to forgive YOUR sins. He, in fact, died on the cross so that sins of all who believe in Him would be forgiven.

What does *Jesus: Forgiver* mean to you? Have you ever shared this with another? What about doing so today?

DAY 11
MEET JESUS
HOPE
1 TIMOTHY 1:1

"This letter is from Paul, an apostle of Christ Jesus, appointed by the command of God our Savior and Christ Jesus, who gives us hope." (1 Timothy 1:1 NLT)

Need hope in your life? Amid sickness, amid suffering, and amid the obstacles of life, Jesus is our hope.

In Jesus..."being justified by his grace we might become heirs according to the hope of eternal life." (Titus 3:7 ESV)

In Jesus..."we do not lose heart. Though our outer self is wasting away, our inner self is being renewed day by day. For this light momentary affliction is preparing for us an eternal weight of glory beyond all comparison." (2 Corinthians 4:16-18 ESV)

In Jesus..."we have also obtained access by faith into this grace in which we stand, and we rejoice in hope of the glory of God. Not only that, but we rejoice in our sufferings, knowing that suffering produces endurance, and endurance produces character, and character produces hope, and hope does not put us to shame, because God's love has been poured into our hearts through the Holy Spirit who has been given to us." (Romans 5:2-5 ESV)

In Jesus..."I can do all things through him who strengthens me." (Philippians 4:13 ESV)

How else do you find hope in Jesus? How have you rested on *Jesus: Hope* in your life? In what ways can Jesus use us to extend His hope to others?

Read Luke 5:27-32.

"Later, as Jesus left the town, he saw a tax collector named Levi sitting at his tax collector's booth. 'Follow me and be my disciple,' Jesus said to him. So Levi got up, left everything, and followed him."
(Luke 5:27-28 NLT)

There is Jesus. There is Matthew. There is Jesus—looked upon (by his "fans") as healer, rabbi, man of God, miracle maker. There is Matthew, tax collector—looked upon by the community as crook, cheat, liar. Polar opposites.

And one day, here is Jesus, crossing the societal lines, "sacrilegious" as ever, approaching the hated, despised tax collector.
Imagine Matthew's surprise.

"Later, Levi held a banquet in his home with Jesus as the guest of honor. Many of Levi's fellow tax collectors and other guests also ate with them. But the Pharisees and their teachers of religious law complained bitterly to Jesus' disciples, 'Why do you eat and drink with such scum?'"
(Luke 5:29- 30 NLT)

There Jesus goes again! What is He doing? How can He be meeting with such people! But this is who Jesus is. Whether to the contagious leper or to the can't-trust-him tax collector, Jesus reaches out. Jesus is the friend of the marginalized.

"I have come to call not those who think they are righteous, but those who know they are sinners and need to repent." (Luke 5:32 NLT)

So how are we to introduce *Jesus: Friend of the Marginalized* to others? Maybe one way is to live as Jesus lived and show the Jesus who lives in us to our community, to those who are marginalized.

James called the early church out on this, "My dear brothers and sisters, how can you claim to have faith in our glorious Lord Jesus Christ if you favor some people over others?" (James 2:1 NLT)

What about you? Where do you have the most room to grow in the area of marginalizing others? What do you have to confess? With Jesus' help, with Him living in you, how may you extend His love to those who are sick, those in need of healing/repenting - physically, emotionally and spiritually?

"Jesus spoke to the people once more and said, 'I am the light of the world. If you follow me, you won't have to walk in darkness, because you will have the light that leads to life.'" (John 8:12 NLT)

Paul wrote in his letter to the Ephesians, "...they are hopelessly confused. Their minds are full of darkness; they wander far from the life God gives because they have closed their minds and hardened their hearts against him. They have no sense of shame. They live for lustful pleasure and eagerly practice every kind of impurity." (Ephesians 4:17b-19 NLT)

How did Paul describe those who walk in darkness? How do you see this in the world around you? How do you see this in the lives of people you know and love?

In Ephesians 4:22-5:7 Paul also described a life living in the light, a life following *Jesus: Light of the World*. **Going through each verse from Ephesians 4:22-5:7, write down one word or phrase on what it means to live in the light. Use the blank area below for this.**

Seem overwhelming at all to live in such a way? Why is that?

Paul went on to say, "For once you were full of darkness, but now you have light from the Lord. So live as people of light! For this light within you produces only what is good and right and true."
(Ephesians 4:8-9 NLT)

What good news do you find in these verses? How are you equipped to actually live as a person of light?

While Jesus called Himself the Light of the World, He also said of those who follow Him, "You are the light of the world—like a city on a hilltop that cannot be hidden. No one lights a lamp and then puts it under a basket. Instead, a lamp is placed on a stand, where it gives light to everyone in the house. In the same way, let your good deeds shine out for all to see, so that everyone will praise your heavenly Father."
(Matthew 5:14-16 NLT)

Taking all of the above into account, how is it that we introduce *Jesus: Light of the World* **to those walking in darkness?**

Read Luke 6:12-16.

The meaning of the word "delegator" has a few variations. It can be used as a noun and as a verb. As a noun it can mean one who acts on behalf of another (like a representative). As a verb, it can mean one who extends powers, functions, responsibilities, etc. out to others (so that these others may serve as agents of the one extending the power).

So here we have Jesus, the Son of God, Creator, choosing men (and not even those most of us would put on our "A"-list) to walk alongside Him, to follow Him, to do as He does, to share with the world the Good News, to change the world. Jesus didn't need to do this. He has all of the power at His finger tips to changes people's lives on His own.

Regardless, and it is a complete mystery, He chose us to help Him with His mission. It is still Jesus ultimately changing people's lives through the power of the Word and the Holy Spirit, but He uses us to share the Good News of Him to others.

What thoughts run through your mind of *Jesus: Delegator*? As agents, how do we represent Him—in effect, introducing who He is and what He is about—to others?

Worship   5 minutes
Whomever is the Worship leader, choose a song that touches you as to who Jesus is. Play the song for the group. Share how you personally **MEET JESUS** through the song.

Devotional Discussion   45 minutes
OPTION 1
Discuss, in order, the questions presented in Day 8 thru 14's devotions.

OPTION 2
Discuss which reading from Day 8 thru 14 spiritually challenged you the most? Why was that? What next step is Jesus calling you to take?

Helping Others MEET JESUS   15 minutes
"As you sent me into the world, so I have sent them into the world."
(John 17:18)

Last week we discussed that during these next several weeks your small group will select, plan, and initiate an effort which will impact the community so that they may **MEET JESUS**.

Here are some next steps:
- Discuss your options.
- Choose your plan.
- Lay out your timeline. What needs to happen by when?
- Who in your group will do what?
- Begin to get things organized.
- Feel free to use blank pages found at the back of booklet for taking notes.
- What are we missing?
- Pray!

Prayer   **20 minutes**

Share a prayer request based on what was discussed during this meeting's Devotional Discussion and/or Helping Others Meet Jesus time. What is that next step in your faith life God is calling you to make? What convicted you from God's Word and/or our discussion of His Word? Please also share a way in which the group may support/encourage you regarding what you've shared. Of course other important matters can be prayed about as well. After all have shared, pray for the person on your left (whether aloud or silently). Pray together in popcorn style (as opposed to going in order around a circle).

Coordinating next week's meeting   **5 minutes**

Study Components	Study Component Leader
Worship	
Devotional Discussion	
Helping Others Meet Jesus	
Prayer	
Coordinating	

<u>**Worship Leader**</u>
Leads worship time during meeting.
<u>**Devotional Discussion Leader**</u>
Leads the Bible Study time, encourages application of God's Word to life.
<u>**Helping Others Meet Jesus Leader**</u>
Leads the effort to impact the community to meet Jesus.
<u>**Prayer Leader**</u>
Leads the group prayer time.
<u>**Coordinating Leader**</u>
Coordinates and reminds who will lead the different meeting components.

"I don't want you to forget, dear brothers and sisters, about our ancestors in the wilderness long ago. All of them were guided by a cloud that moved ahead of them, and all of them walked through the sea on dry ground. In the cloud and in the sea, all of them were baptized as followers of Moses. All of them ate the same spiritual food, and all of them drank the same spiritual water. For they drank from the spiritual rock that traveled with them, and that rock was Christ." (1 Corinthians 10:1-4 NLT)

Been through some shaky ground in life? Loss of a loved one? Diagnosed with cancer? Laid off from work? Depressed? Worried? Some of these experiences feel shaky because they carry with them pain, uncertainty of the future, lack of protection. It is in these times we need a sure and steady foundation. We need someone strong in our lives when we are weak. We need provision instead of always being the provider (for others or for ourselves).

Thankfully, we have *Jesus: Rock*. He is the One to whom we can count on through all of life's difficult moments.

Psalm 18:2 (NLT) captures this beautifully,

> "The Lord is my rock, my fortress, and my savior;
> my God is my rock, in whom I find protection.
> He is my shield, the power that saves me,
> and my place of safety."

Describe a time in your life where you drank from *Jesus: Rock* for your provision, health and protection? What did it mean to you? To whom may you share your story? To whom may you introduce *Jesus: Rock*?

Read Luke 6:20-23.

Need blessing in your life? Jesus blesses.

He shared with His disciples and the crowd which followed Him,

"God blesses you who are poor, for the Kingdom of God is yours. God blesses you who are hungry now, for you will be satisfied. God blesses you who weep now, for in due time you will laugh." (Luke 6:20-21 NLT)

Are you feeling poor - whether financially, spiritually, physically? Jesus blesses you.

Are you hungry—whether your stomach is actually groaning or you long for relationship? Jesus blesses you.

Are you mourning—whether over the loss of a loved one or a trial a friend is experiencing? Jesus blesses you (and your friend).

Like the milk ad, "got blessing?" No matter what we are going through, Jesus' blessing is there. It is given freely to us. This is who He is. This is what He does.

Now when one is blessed, the trial, the hardship, the mourning may not necessarily evaporate. Yet one blessed receives a new or renewed countenance. Jeremiah provided a snapshot of one on the receiving end of God's blessing:

> "But blessed is the one who trusts in the Lord,
> whose confidence is in him.
> They will be like a tree planted by the water
> that sends out its roots by the stream.
> It does not fear when heat comes;
> its leaves are always green.
> It has no worries in a year of drought
> and never fails to bear fruit."
> (Jeremiah 17:7-8 NIV)

Above ground the heat may come. On ground level the drought may continue. But deep down, the roots are connected to a wellspring that never dries up. These roots are continually fed with confidence in the One providing blessing, protection, community, nourishment, all that we truly need.

As we look to **_Jesus: Blesser_**, we can direct others to Him. In the letters (epistles) found in the New Testament, we see blessings given by writers to their recipients (to us).

Paul ended his letter to the Philippians simply, "The grace of the Lord Jesus Christ be with your spirit. Amen." (Philippians 4:23 NIV)

In what ways may God use us (use you) to be extenders of Jesus' blessings to others—to the poor, to the hungry, to the sad?

"I am writing to Titus, my true son in the faith that we share. May God the Father and Christ Jesus our Savior give you grace and peace."
(Titus 1:4 NLT)

Pop culture definitely grasps the idea of "savior." It is especially apparent in comics and super-hero movies. I noticed this right away in the first 5 minutes of the cartoon movie *Planet Hulk*. As Hulk is blasted in a spacecraft out of Earth's atmosphere, an alien from a distant planet is seen praying (to whomever) for a savior to save his people. And boom, crash land...here comes the Hulk!

Unlike pop culture, Jesus is the real deal. He is the Savior of the world. For our sins, which kept us separated from our Holy God, Jesus came into our world (sent by God the Father) to take our punishment, to pay our penalty, to die for our sins...so that we may live, not perish, and have eternal life.

What does *Jesus: Savior* mean to you? Where else in our culture do people look to saviors? Sports? Politics? Give some specific examples.

Not to diminish or downcast such individuals' accomplishments and possibly selfless service, but how do such folks pale in comparison to *Jesus: Savior*?

What are other ways, examples, we can introduce *Jesus: Savior*, the real deal, to our communities, to our friends, to our neighbors?

Read Luke 6:27-36.

[Jesus said,] "But to you who are willing to listen, I say, love your enemies! Do good to those who hate you. Bless those who curse you. Pray for those who hurt you." (Luke 6:27-28 NLT)

Jesus: Enemy-lover. Sounds quite jarring. I could have referred to Him as ***Jesus: Lover of Enemies,*** but maybe ***Jesus: Enemy-lover*** pushes the point further.

Paul wrote, "But God showed his great love for us by sending Christ to die for us while we were still sinners." (Romans 5:8 NLT) "While we were still sinners." As sinners we go against and rebel against God, basically behaving as His enemy. But God sent Jesus to save us any way. It wasn't because we did good works. It was simply because He loved us.

As we look at God's Word, the God of the Old Testament is the same as the God of the New. Recall the story of Jonah. It begins, "The Lord gave this message to Jonah son of Amittai: 'Get up and go to the great city of Nineveh. Announce my judgment against it because I have seen how wicked its people are.'" (Jonah 1:1-2 NLT) If you are familiar with the story, Jonah didn't want to go. And he had good reason for feeling that way. It could be argued that the Ninevehites were the worst of the worst of the worst of God's enemies.

Meet one of Ninevah's cruelest kings. This will give you a sense of Nineveh, of their evilness and what Jonah would have known about them. WARNING: THIS IS GRAPHIC!

The following was written by King Ashurnasirpal II (883-859 BC). He wrote, "I flayed (the skin from) as many nobles as had rebelled against me (and) draped their skins over the pile (of corpses)...I cut off the heads of their fighters (and) built (with them) a tower before their city. I burnt their adolescent boys (and) girls...I captured many troops alive: I cut off their arms (and) hands; I cut off of others their noses, ears, and extremities. I gouged out the eyes of many troops. I made one pile of the living (and) one of the heads. I hung their heads on trees around the city." [from James K. Bruckner, Jonah, Nahum, Habakkuk, Zephaniah : The NIV Application Commentary from Biblical Text– to Contemporary Life, Niv Application Commentary(Grand Rapids, Mich.: Zondervan, 2004), 29.]

What familiarity do you find in our world today?

Does Jesus still love those who are against Him?

How does God call us to do as He did/does? How does Jesus call us to love our enemies, introducing them to His incredible love and grace?

"But to those called by God to salvation, both Jews and Gentiles, Christ is the power of God and the wisdom of God." (1 Corinthians 1:24 NLT)

A number of years ago the Christian craze was "WWJD"—What Would Jesus Do. WWJD was printed on everything. Wristbands. Bumper stickers. Pens and pencils. You name it!

Whether you thought it was over-marketed or not, I definitely understand the crux behind the slogan. Jesus was the wisest man who ever walked the earth. Of course, there was King Solomon, but Solomon was only a man. Jesus was God Himself.

Thanks to some fellas named, Matthew, Mark, Luke and John (not to forget the source of their inspiration—the Holy Spirit), we are able to look at how Jesus lived. In their gospel accounts, we can see what Jesus did and said. So, want to know the wisdom of Jesus? Need wisdom in your life? Read the gospels.

Carl Medearis in *Speaking of Jesus*, wrote, "Now I tell people that if you want to get to know Jesus, the actual person, then read the four Gospels. Read them until they become part of you. Eat and breathe them."

Throughout this 40-day devotional, we've been talking a lot about introducing people to Jesus. What better way to introduce people to Jesus than when we get to know Him better each day, regularly reading the accounts of His life on earth.

What is your next step in being either introduced or re-introduced to Jesus through the Gospels of Matthew, Mark, Luke or John? Read a chapter a day? Read one gospel account a month? What is a doable plan for you?

Read Luke 6:46-49.

[Jesus said] "I will show you what it's like when someone comes to me, listens to my teaching, and then follows it. It is like a person building a house who digs deep and lays the foundation on solid rock."
(Luke 6:47-48a NLT)

Jesus is that sure, steady ground. It is on Him and on His Word we find stability and peace no matter what is swirling around us.

"When the floodwaters rise and break against that house, it stands firm because it is well built." (Luke 6:48b NLT)

What do those who do not follow Jesus attempt to stand on? What do they count on for safety? How have those attempts been tested successfully and proved long lasting?

Or is this what they find?

"But anyone who hears and doesn't obey is like a person who builds a house without a foundation. When the floods sweep down against that house, it will collapse into a heap of ruins." (Luke 6:49 NLT)

How may you introduce *Jesus: Foundation* to those in need of an actual firm ground to stand on? You may start with sharing how Jesus has been your foundation.

Read John 15:1-8.

[Jesus said] "Yes, I am the vine; you are the branches." (John 15:5a NLT)

"Remain in me, and I will remain in you." (John 15:4a NLT)

What are 3 ways you would describe a vine to someone?
-
-
-

What are 3 ways you would describe a branch to someone?
-
-
-

When you think of Jesus as the vine and His followers as the branches, what 3 images or thoughts come to mind?
-
-
-

What are 3 ways you've experienced Jesus being your vine?
-
-
-

If you've completed the above, you are ready to introduce *Jesus: Vine* to another.

Worship 5 minutes
Whomever is the Worship leader, choose a song that touches you as to who Jesus is. Play the song for the group. Share how you personally **MEET JESUS** through the song.

Devotional Discussion 45 minutes
OPTION 1
Discuss, in order, the questions presented in Day 15 thru 21's devotions.

OPTION 2
Discuss which reading from Day 15 thru 21 spiritually challenged you the most? Why was that? What next step is Jesus calling you to take?

Helping Others MEET JESUS 15 minutes
"As you sent me into the world, so I have sent them into the world."
(John 17:18)

Continue planning your **HELPING OTHERS MEET JESUS** initiative. What details still need to be taken care of? Who are those outside of your group, maybe even your friends who do not-yet-know Jesus, you could invite to be a part of your plans?

Prayer   **20 minutes**

Share a prayer request based on what was discussed during this meeting's Devotional Discussion and/or Helping Others Meet Jesus time. What is that next step in your faith life God is calling you to make? What convicted you from God's Word and/or our discussion of His Word? Please also share a way in which the group may support/encourage you regarding what you've shared. Of course other important matters can be prayed about as well. After all have shared, pray for the person on your left (whether aloud or silently). Pray together in popcorn style (as opposed to going in order around a circle).

Coordinating next week's meeting   **5 minutes**

Study Components	Study Component Leader
Worship	
Devotional Discussion	
Helping Others Meet Jesus	
Prayer	
Coordinating	

<u>Worship Leader</u>
Leads worship time during meeting.
<u>Devotional Discussion Leader</u>
Leads the Bible Study time, encourages application of God's Word to life.
<u>Helping Others Meet Jesus Leader</u>
Leads the effort to impact the community to meet Jesus.
<u>Prayer Leader</u>
Leads the group prayer time.
<u>Coordinating Leader</u>
Coordinates and reminds who will lead the different meeting components.

Read Luke 7:1-10.

"So Jesus went with them. But just before they arrived at the house, the officer [of the sick slave whom Jesus was asked to heal) sent some friends to say, 'Lord, don't trouble yourself by coming to my home, for I am not worthy of such an honor. I am not worthy to come and meet you. Just say the word from where you are, and my servant will be healed. I know this because I am under the authority of my superior officers, and I have authority over my soldiers. I only need to say, 'Go,' and they go, or 'Come,' and they come. And if I say to my slaves, 'Do this,' they do it."
(Luke 7:6-8 NLT)

This Roman officer knew of Jesus' authority. The rumors were true.

In this 40-day devotional, every other day, we've been reading through the Book of Luke. We are only in Luke 7 and already have seen these examples of Jesus' authority distinguished:
- Resisted the devil's temptations. Luke 4:1-13.
- Filled with the Holy Spirit's power. Luke 4:14a.
- Reports of His power flooded the region. Luke 4:14b.
- Praised for His teaching in the synagogues. Luke 4:15.
- Everyone spoke well of Him and were amazed by Him. Luke 4:22.
- Cast out a demon from a young man. Including the people's exclamation "What authority and power this man's words possess!" Luke 4:35-36.
- Healed many. Luke 4:39, 5:13, 5:24, 6:10, 6:19.
- Immediate response from His disciples to follow Him. Luke 5:10-11, 5:27-28, 6:12-16.
- Authority over the Sabbath. Luke 6:5.

Jesus has the same authority today. And the above list only scratches the surface. These accounts of Jesus' authority come from less than 1/3 of the entire Book of Luke.

What authority of Jesus do you point to in your life, in the world around us? How is Jesus' authority good news to all? Along with the Word (like what we are reading in Luke), how may we introduce *Jesus: Authority* to those around us?

The rest of the above story from Luke 7..."When Jesus heard this, he was amazed. Turning to the crowd that was following him, he said, 'I tell you, I haven't seen faith like this in all Israel!' And when the officer's friends returned to his house, they found the slave completely healed."
(Luke 7:9-10 NLT)

me·di·a·tor (mēdē͵ādər) / noun – a go-between; one who gets in the middle of two parties for the purpose of reconciliation.

Another word for go-between is bridge. If there is a great divide between point A and point B, we need a bridge to reconcile that gap. That is what Jesus is...our bridge to God, our mediator with God the Father.

"For, There is one God and one Mediator who can reconcile God and humanity—the man Christ Jesus." (1 Timothy 2:5 NLT)

Review the bridge analogy found at *http://bridgeanalogy.blogspot.com/*. **Become familiar with it. Practice it with another follower of Jesus. Learn to share it verbally. Learn to share it by actually drawing it out. Take turns and try this in the safety of a small group meeting.**

This is one way to introduce *Jesus: Mediator* to another. As you practice it, you become that much more equipped, prepared, and ready when given the opportunity to share it with one who is far from God.

DAY 24
MEET JESUS
PROPHET
LUKE 7:11-17

Read Luke 7:11-17.

"Great fear swept the crowd, and they praised God, saying, 'A mighty prophet has risen among us,' and 'God has visited his people today.'" (Luke 7:16 NLT)

Christian Cyclopedia (http://cyclopedia.lcms.org/) defines the word prophet, "in Scripture a prophet is a divinely inspired forth-teller (1 Sm 10:6; Jer 1:2; Eze 1:1; Hos 1:1; 1 Ptr 1:11; 2 Ptr 1:21) who rebukes sin (2 Sm 12; Is 58:1; Eze 3:17; Mi 3:8), shows God's mercy (Is 40; 53), and in gen., proclaims messages of God (Ex 4:14–15; 7:1–2: Eze 11; Heb 1:1–2)."

We see all of these prophetic qualities in Jesus' life.
- Rebuked sin (John 8:11)
- Showed God's mercy (Matthew 5:3-12)
- Proclaimed messages of God
   (The Sermon on the Mount - Matthew 5:13-7:29)

Throughout the Old Testament, God's prophets forth-told of the coming Messiah, the one who would come and save God's people.

Jesus forth-told of this as well.

"Some of the people who lived in Jerusalem started to ask each other, 'Could our leaders possibly believe that he is the Messiah? But how could he be? For we know where this man comes from. When the Messiah comes, he will simply appear; no one will know where he comes from.' While Jesus was teaching in the Temple, he called out, 'Yes, you know me, and you know where I come from. But I'm not here on my own. The one who sent me is true, and you don't know him. But I know him because I come from him, and he sent me to you.'" (John 7:25a, 26b-29 NLT)

What separates Jesus from all the other prophets is that Jesus came to the world and forth-told the Good News of Himself.

"For this is how God loved the world: He gave his one and only Son, so that everyone who believes in him will not perish but have eternal life. God sent his Son into the world not to judge the world, but to save the world through him." (John 3:16-17 NLT)

Where else in God's Word do we find *Jesus: Prophet*? What was people's reaction to the prophecy He shared? Who were offended? Who were afraid? Whose lives were forever changed, saved by God, not to perish but to have eternal life with our Loving God?

> "And the news about Jesus spread throughout Judea and the surrounding countryside." (Luke 7:17 NLT)

How may we spread the news and introduce *Jesus: Prophet* to others? How may we reveal from God's Word that Jesus wasn't just a man who taught great wisdom and did kind things, but that He was (is) God Himself, who came to us (not us to Him) to save us from sin and death?

DAY 25
MEET JESUS
DELIVERER
ROMANS 11:25-27

[Paul wrote, quoting the prophet Isaiah] "I do not want you to be ignorant of this mystery, brothers and sisters, so that you may not be conceited: Israel has experienced a hardening in part until the full number of the Gentiles has come in, and in this way all Israel will be saved. As it is written:

> 'The deliverer will come from Zion;
> he will turn godlessness away from Jacob.
> And this is my covenant with them
> when I take away their sins.'"
> (Romans 11:25-27 NIV)

The deliver who would come, who came, is Jesus.

On Day 17, we met *Jesus: Savior*. Savior and Deliverer are similar descriptions for who Jesus is. We looked at *Jesus: Savior* with a fairly broad stroke. Today, we will look at *Jesus: Deliverer* in a more intimate way as expressed in Psalm 40. Here is a personal testimony as to what Deliverer means from Jesus' great, great, great, great (on and on) grandfather David:

> I waited patiently for the Lord;
> he turned to me and heard my cry.
> He lifted me out of the slimy pit,
> out of the mud and mire;
> he set my feet on a rock
> and gave me a firm place to stand.
> He put a new song in my mouth,
>
> a hymn of praise to our God.
> Many will see and fear the Lord
> and put their trust in him.

I proclaim your saving acts in the great assembly;
I do not seal my lips, Lord,
as you know.
I do not hide your righteousness in my heart;
I speak of your faithfulness and your saving help.
I do not conceal your love and your faithfulness

from the great assembly.
But may all who seek you
rejoice and be glad in you;
may those who long for your saving help always say,
"The Lord is great!"
But as for me, I am poor and needy;
may the Lord think of me.
You are my help and my deliverer;
you are my God
(Psalm 40:1-3, 9-10, 16-17a NIV)

What words would you choose to explain what *Jesus: Deliverer* means to you? As a witness, with whom may you share your testimony?

Read Luke 7:18-50.

"John's two disciples found Jesus and said to him, 'John the Baptist sent us to ask, "Are you the Messiah we've been expecting, or should we keep looking for someone else?" At that very time, Jesus cured many people of their diseases, illnesses, and evil spirits, and he restored sight to many who were blind. Then he told John's disciples, 'Go back to John and tell him what you have seen and heard—the blind see, the lame walk, the lepers are cured, the deaf hear, the dead are raised to life, and the Good News is being preached to the poor. And tell him, 'God blesses those who do not turn away because of me.'" (Luke 7:20-23 NLT)

In this account Jesus gave the long answer. He responded to the question of John's disciples with the evidence of His actions. In John 4:25-26 (NLT), Jesus was more succinct, "The woman said to him, 'I know that Messiah is coming (he who is called Christ). When he comes, he will tell us all things.' Jesus said to her, 'I who speak to you am he.'"

Messiah means "anointed one" as in oil poured on one. Another snapshot of *Jesus: Messiah* found in Luke 7:46-50 (NLT):

[Jesus speaking to Simon the Pharisee] "'You neglected the courtesy of olive oil to anoint my head, but she has anointed my feet with rare perfume. I tell you, her sins—and they are many—have been forgiven, so she has shown me much love. But a person who is forgiven little shows only little love.' Then Jesus said to the woman, 'Your sins are forgiven.' The men at the table said among themselves, 'Who is this man, that he goes around forgiving sins?' And Jesus said to the woman, 'Your faith has saved you; go in peace.'"

Christian Cyclopedia (http://cyclopedia.lcms.org/) reports, "The OT [Old Testament] offers hope of a messiah-king after the image of David (e.g., Ps 2; 18; 20; 21; 45). It also refers to Messiah in such terms as the coming Judge (e.g., Is 42:1–4), Ruler of Israel (e.g., 2 Sm 7:13; Zch 9:9; Ps 2:6; Dn 9:25), Wonderful, Counselor, Mighty God, Everlasting Father, Prince of Peace (Is 9:6; cf. Ju 13:18)." Jesus filled the hope of all of these.

Most importantly for us..."who is this man, that goes around forgiving sins?" Answer: **Jesus: Messiah**.

Many movies include a messiah theme (all taken from the Bible). In these movies, the characters look to the One who would come to save, redeem, make things right again. One could look at *Star Wars* Episodes I-III as Old Testament. And Episodes IV-VI as New Testament. In Episodes I-II, the Jedi were looking to for One who would provide order to the universe. Ultimately, in Episode VI (with a rocky road of evil and destruction along the way) that One was Anikan Skywalker (aka Darth Vader) who defeated the evil emperor.

How is Jesus the One to you? How has he saved, redeemed, put things right in your life? How may you express this to another?

DAY 27
MEET JESUS
GOD
JOHN 1:1

"In the beginning the Word already existed. The Word was with God, and the Word was God." (John 1:1 NLT)

The "Word" John was referring to is Jesus. So John 1:1 could also be said, "In the beginning Jesus already existed. Jesus was with God, and Jesus was God."

Many religions and religious leaders look at Jesus positively. This can be said of Gandhi (Hinduism), Muhammad (Islam), the Dalai Lama (Buddhism), to name a few. But considering Jesus as God is another thing. And *Jesus: God* is exactly what separates those who follow Jesus from all other world religions.

As mentioned in previous daily devotions, in ALL world religions, man needs to do something on his/her own part to obtain salvation, eternal life with God. Those who follow Jesus know from God's Word that there is nothing man can do to earn salvation. As Paul wrote, "For everyone has sinned; we all fall short of God's glorious standard." (Romans 3:23 NLT) Because of us always falling short, we needed an external source to save us; eternal life with God is something we can never achieve by our good works. And if we are truly honest with ourselves and did the counting, how could we ever really count more good works done by us in a lifespan over our evil actions and thoughts? So this is what God did...He sent Himself to earth to save us by the death and resurrection of Jesus Christ. This act of *Jesus: God* is the epitome of the word grace.

Other religions use the word grace, but when you look deeply enough there are always strings attached whereby negating what grace is supposed to mean (love with no strings).

How do you find what God did in sending His Son (Himself) as true grace ("undeserved love", "love without strings attached")? How has God's grace impacted your life? How may we introduce God's grace as known in *Jesus: God* to another?

DAY 28 — MEET JESUS STORM-CLAMER — LUKE 8:22-25

Read Luke 8:22-25.

"But soon a fierce storm came down on the lake. The boat was filling with water, and they were in real danger. The disciples went and woke him up, shouting, 'Master, Master, we're going to drown!' When Jesus woke up, he rebuked the wind and the raging waves. Suddenly the storm stopped and all was calm." (Luke 8:23b-24 NLT)

What storms in life have you faced? How have you reacted to them?

If the disciples had already seen incredible miracles of Jesus, why would they have worried about a storm when Jesus was with them?

Like the disciples, maybe we all need the reminder. The disciples forgot the powerful force that was with them in the boat. We who follow Jesus today, who have Jesus living in us, forget the fact as well.

Thus the need for Paul's reminders to the early church.

He reminded the Corinthians, "Surely you know that Jesus Christ is among you." (2 Corinthians 2:5 NLT)

He reminded the Galatians, "It is no longer I who live, but Christ lives in me." (Galatians 2:20 NLT)

He reminded the Colossians, "And this is the secret: Christ lives in you. This gives you assurance of sharing his glory." (Colossians 1:27 NLT)

The good news in the above account: when Jesus said to His disciples, "Where is your faith?", He said this after He calmed the storm. He didn't wait for them to get their "act together." He heard their desperate plea, "Master, Master...", answered it, and did so immediately.

Looking back over those storms you've experienced, how did you see *Jesus: Storm-calmer* in action?

In your words how would you explain storms, faith, fear and trust in Jesus to another, especially one going through their own storm of life?

Worship   5 minutes
Whomever is the Worship leader, choose a song that touches you as to who Jesus is. Play the song for the group. Share how you personally **MEET JESUS** through the song.

Devotional Discussion   45 minutes
OPTION 1
Discuss, in order, the questions presented in Day 22 thru 28's devotions.

OPTION 2
Discuss which reading from Day 22 thru 28 spiritually challenged you the most? Why was that? What next step is Jesus calling you to take?

Helping Others MEET JESUS   15 minutes
"As you sent me into the world, so I have sent them into the world."
(John 17:18)

What details remain? What needs to be taken care of to fulfill your plans? Review who is doing what and talk through any other logistics.

Prayer   **20 minutes**

Share a prayer request based on what was discussed during this meeting's Devotional Discussion and/or Helping Others Meet Jesus time. What is that next step in your faith life God is calling you to make? What convicted you from God's Word and/or our discussion of His Word? Please also share a way in which the group may support/encourage you regarding what you've shared. Of course other important matters can be prayed about as well. After all have shared, pray for the person on your left (whether aloud or silently). Pray together in popcorn style (as opposed to going in order around a circle).

Coordinating next week's meeting   **5 minutes**

Study Components	Study Component Leader
Worship	
Devotional Discussion	
Helping Others Meet Jesus	
Prayer	
Coordinating	

<u>***Worship Leader***</u>
Leads worship time during meeting.
<u>***Devotional Discussion Leader***</u>
Leads the Bible Study time, encourages application of God's Word to life.
<u>***Helping Others Meet Jesus Leader***</u>
Leads the effort to impact the community to meet Jesus.
<u>***Prayer Leader***</u>
Leads the group prayer time.
<u>***Coordinating Leader***</u>
Coordinates and reminds who will lead the different meeting components.

"For sin is the sting that results in death, and the law gives sin its power. But thank God! He gives us victory over sin and death through our Lord Jesus Christ." (1 Corinthians 15:56-57 NLT)

What else does God's Word say on *Jesus: Victor*?

- "If God is for us, who can ever be against us? Since he did not spare even his own Son but gave him up for us all, won't he also give us everything else?" (Romans 8:31b-32 NLT)
- [Jesus said] "I have told you all this so that you may have peace in me. Here on earth you will have many trials and sorrows. But take heart, because I have overcome the world." (John 16:33 NLT)
- "The temptations in your life are no different from what others experience. And God is faithful. He will not allow the temptation to be more than you can stand. When you are tempted, he will show you a way out so that you can endure." (1 Corinthians 10:13 NLT)
- "Christ suffered for our sins once for all time. He never sinned, but he died for sinners to bring you safely home to God. He suffered physical death, but he was raised to life in the Spirit." (1 Peter 3:18 NLT)

What does *Jesus: Victor* mean for those who follow Him?

- "A final word: Be strong in the Lord and in his mighty power." (Ephesians 6:10 NLT)

- "For every child of God defeats this evil world, and we achieve this victory through our faith." (1 John 5:4 NLT)

What other verses speak of the victory we have in Jesus?

How have you experienced *Jesus: Victor* in your life?

Who in your life is being trampled upon by sin, addiction, trouble [if responding to this in a small group, it is not necessary to share names]? How may you encourage this person by introducing them to *Jesus: Victor*?

Read Luke 8:26-39.

"What have you to do with me, Jesus, Son of the Most High God?" (Luke 8:28 NLT). Yes, even demons knew who Jesus was.

On day 27, we met ***Jesus: God***. This is true. And He is also the Son of God. This may seem like a confusing concept. The Christian Church believes in the Holy Trinity—Father, Son and Holy Spirit. One God, but three in one. On the simpler side of things you can think of the different hats in life you may wear. For me, I'm Craig:Brother. Craig: Dad. Craig: Son. But I'm still simply...Craig.

You won't find the specific word "Trinity" in the Bible but you will find the teachings of the Trinity in God's Word. Just one example is Matthew 28:19 (NLT), "Go therefore and make disciples of all nations, baptizing them in the name of the Father and of the Son and of the Holy Spirit."

Below is the Nicene Creed, accepted by all Christian churches, all denominations (Lutheran, Catholic, Methodist, Assembly of God, etc.) which explain what we believe of God, which includes ***Jesus: Son of God***:

I believe in one God, the Father Almighty, maker of heaven and earth and of all things visible and invisible.

And in one Lord Jesus Christ, the only-begotten Son of God, begotten of His Father before all worlds, God of God, Light of Light, very God of very God, begotten, not made, being of one substance with the Father, by whom all things were made; who for us men and for our salvation came down from heaven and was incarnate by the Holy Spirit of the virgin Mary and was made man; and was crucified also for us under Pontius Pilate. He suffered and was buried. And the third day He rose again according to the Scriptures and ascended into heaven and sits at the right hand of the Father. And He will come again with glory to judge both the living and the dead, whose kingdom will have no end.

And I believe in the Holy Spirit, the Lord and giver of life, who proceeds from the Father and the Son, who with the Father and the Son together is worshiped and glorified, who spoke by the prophets. And I believe in one holy Christian and apostolic Church I acknowledge one Baptism for the remission of sins, and I look for the resurrection of the dead and the life of the world to come.

Amen.

Now, back to the account in Luke 8:26-39. What do we see of ***Jesus: Son of God***?
- He has power over demons and can cast them out.
- People feared Jesus.
- Even though most wanted Jesus to leave from them, one man didn't. "The man from whom the demons had gone begged that he might be with him, but Jesus sent him away, saying, 'Return to your home, and declare how much God has done for you.' And he went away, proclaiming throughout the whole city how much Jesus had done for him." (Luke 8:38-39 NLT)

Regardless of the source (when the man was demon-possessed), it is still a good question we can ask of ***Jesus: Son of God***. "What have you to do with me, Jesus, Son of the Most High God?" **What could it mean to ask Jesus of this each day of your life? What would be the impact…on you… on the lives of the people around you?**

In what specific ways may we return to our homes, declare how much Jesus has done for us, and proclaim this throughout the community we live in?

"So if the Son sets you free, you are truly free." (John 8:36 NLT)

Because of what Jesus did on the cross, died and rose again, we are free from the chains of sin and death. We have this assurance!

We have this assurance even in the times we stumble and fall. Paul wrote of this to the church in Rome, "I have discovered this principle of life—that when I want to do what is right, I inevitably do what is wrong. I love God's law with all my heart. But there is another power within me that is at war with my mind. This power makes me a slave to the sin that is still within me. Oh, what a miserable person I am! Who will free me from this life that is dominated by sin and death? Thank God! The answer is in Jesus Christ our Lord." (Romans 7:21-25a NLT)

Again, be assured. Jesus is our Chain-breaker!

How do you live today in the presence of *Jesus: Chain-breaker*? How do you experience the freedom found in Christ and in Him alone? How does Jesus equip you for your day and the challenges, temptations, and trials you face?

Some words to encourage you from Lauren Daigle's song *How Can It Be*:

> I am guilty
> Ashamed of what I've done, what I've become
> These hands are dirty
> I dare not lift them up to the Holy One
> You plead my cause, you right my wrongs
> You break my chains, you overcome
> You gave your life, to give me mine
> You say that I am free

How may we encourage and introduce others to the good news found in *Jesus: Chain-breaker*?

DAY 32 — MEET JESUS — MULTIPLIER — JOHN 8:36

Read Luke 9:10-17.

"Jesus said, 'You feed them.'

'But we have only five loaves of bread and two fish,' they answered. 'Or are you expecting us to go and buy enough food for this whole crowd?' For there were about 5,000 men there.

Jesus replied, 'Tell them to sit down in groups of about fifty each.' So the people all sat down. Jesus took the five loaves and two fish, looked up toward heaven, and blessed them. Then, breaking the loaves into pieces, he kept giving the bread and fish to the disciples so they could distribute it to the people. They all ate as much as they wanted, and afterward, the disciples picked up twelve baskets of leftovers!" (Luke 9:10-17 NLT)

What we see as limitations, Jesus sees as possibilities. Later in the book of Luke, Jesus said, "What is impossible for people is possible with God." (Luke 18:27 NLT)

A number of years ago I launched a Friday morning men's group in the fall. It started with me and 2 other guys. We had a vision of multiplying so that we could connect more men into Christian community. The hope was to multiply into 2 groups within one year. A good vision.

But Jesus thought bigger.

The group met weekly but started slowly. This may not be exactly how it turned out, but it was something like…first week it was me and Gary; Rocky forgot or slept in. Second week it was me and Rocky; Gary forgot or slept in. Third week, I missed and it was just Rocky and Gary. This went on for weeks. Our vision of multiplying into 2 groups in one year wasn't looking to good.

And then Jesus did His thing.

The group grew and grew. By late spring we had 18 guys showing up every Friday and we multiplied (the original group still meeting on Friday and the new group meeting on Thursday). This happened 6 months earlier than we had originally visioned. Then just a couple of months later one thing led to another and a second Thursday group multiplied off of the fairly new Thursday group. Later in the summer a couple of the guys felt the call to launch a Saturday morning group. And they did.

What resulted? Jesus took our original vision of multiplying in one year and QUADRUPLED IT!

Epilogue: Two weeks after the Saturday group launched, I was at our church campus for a morning leadership meeting. A random fella, not from our church, walked in the building around 7:30 am. He had noticed our church for a while and was looking for information about who we were and how he could get connected. (Why at 7:30 am...I don't know!) I gave him a little tour and then asked, "You know, we have a men's group that just began meeting a few minutes ago. Would you like to check it out?" He replied, "Sure." I walked him into the room and the guys welcomed him in with open arms! The man became an active, weekly member of the group.

How could have things been different for the man if I didn't have this almost instant way of connecting him? Not sure. But it seemed the timing of this Saturday morning group launching was just right...just as Jesus had planned, through His multiplication efforts.

How have you seen *Jesus: Multiplier* active in your life? How has He flipped what seemed impossible to being possible and more so? What does *Jesus: Multiplier* mean for our lives?

What could *Jesus: Multiplier* mean for those in your life, who only see what is before them and not what is possible with Jesus' hand in it (especially when the dream/vision is about Jesus' mission to reach more people with His love)?

Read Luke 10:25-37.

Day 33 of **MEET JESUS** and I'm just getting into *Jesus: Teacher*. Shows how multi-faceted Jesus our Lord and Savior is.

"One day an expert in religious law stood up to test Jesus by asking him this question: 'Teacher, what should I do to inherit eternal life?'" (Luke 10:25 NLT)

It is interesting enough to note that an expert in religious law acknowledges Jesus as "Teacher". And, at least from the context in Luke, we are not seeing a snarky Pharisee attempting to trip Jesus up (as if that could ever happen). Instead we have a genuine scene of teacher and pupil.

A good teacher helps his/her student to think and grapple with the challenging questions in life, not just spoon feed answers.
Notice how many questions Jesus asked in the dialogue. **What did the expert in religious law learn through Jesus' teaching and questions? What did you learn?**

AN ASSIGNMENT. Go through one of the other gospel accounts (Matthew, Mark or John) and look for questions Jesus asked. From those questions, 1) what do you find Jesus teaching the person/people being asked and 2) what is He teaching you?

How may you connect one in need of answers to *Jesus: Teacher* who has all of the crucial answers and all of the right questions we need to guide our lives?

Read Luke 10:38-42.

"Martha was distracted by the big dinner she was preparing. She came to Jesus and said, 'Lord, doesn't it seem unfair to you that my sister just sits here while I do all the work? Tell her to come and help me.'"
(Luke 10:38-42 NLT)

Busyness for the sake of busyness...the great distraction, the great excuse, the great relationship stunter.

How do you relate—whether being the one sucked into busyness or the casualty of another's busyness? Why is it so easy for busyness to take over life?

Now Jesus did call us to live a life for Him. He commissioned us in Matthew 28:19 (NLT) to "go and make disciples of all the nations, baptizing them in the name of the Father and the Son and the Holy Spirit." There is some "doing" involved in this. It does take work. It will take our time to go and make disciples.

But we'll never be most effective in our "doing" if we are never just sitting, resting, reclining with Jesus. In these times, we are renewed, refreshed, re-energized, and reminded of His great love for us.

Where is the busyness in Psalm 23:1-3 (NLT)?

> "The Lord is my shepherd;
> I have all that I need.
> He lets me rest in green meadows;
> he leads me beside peaceful streams.
> He renews my strength.
> He guides me along right paths,
> bringing honor to his name."

There isn't any. In these times we are the recipients of His action where "He lets", "He leads", "He renews" and "He guides".

So as we are introducing Jesus to another, do we unintentionally introduce **Jesus: Taskmaster**? Are we over busy in our Christian lives to not spend time with people? Are we in fifty-million church meetings, functions, etc. during the week, where people outside of us would think, "Who needs that? I already have enough stress in life?"

Or can we show others **Jesus: One With Whom To Waste Our Time**? One with whom to sit at His feet. One with home to slow the pace of life down. One with whom to remember the truly important aspects of life.

"But the Lord said to her, 'My dear Martha, you are worried and upset over all these details! There is only one thing worth being concerned about. Mary has discovered it, and it will not be taken away from her.'" (Luke 10:41-42 NLT)

After that time spent with Jesus, I think Mary could have sung the refrain from Brad Paisley's *Time Well Wasted*:

> "It was time well wasted
> And there's no way I trade a few more things
> that I could've crossed off my list
> For a day I'll never forget
> No, I didn't get a thing done
> But I sure soaked up every minute of the memory we were makin'
> And I count it all as time well wasted"

In what ways could you begin to waste more time with Jesus?

DAY 35 — MEET JESUS PRAYER-ANSWERER — LUKE 11:1-13

Read Luke 11:1-13.

Jesus said, "And so I tell you, keep on asking, and you will receive what you ask for. Keep on seeking, and you will find. Keep on knocking, and the door will be opened to you. For everyone who asks, receives. Everyone who seeks, finds. And to everyone who knocks, the door will be opened." (Luke 11:9-10 NLT)

I don't know about you, but when I read, "keep on asking, and you will receive what you ask for", I am incredibly encouraged; I am given hope. This is hope that only God can grant. The answer may come soon. The answer may come slower than I wish. But as Paul instructed the Thessalonians, "Never stop praying." (1 Thessalonians 5:17 NLT). Jesus is our hope when we lift our prayers to Him.

How has God answered your prayers in the past? Did the answers come quick or take some time? What did God's answers mean to your faith in Him?

How may you share the hope of *Jesus: Prayer-answerer* with another— especially one going through a difficult, trying time? In what ways could you share your story and experience?

"So if you sinful people know how to give good gifts to your children, how much more will your heavenly Father give the Holy Spirit to those who ask him." (Luke 11:13 NLT)

Worship 5 minutes

Whomever is the Worship leader, choose a song that touches you as to who Jesus is. Play the song for the group. Share how you personally **MEET JESUS** through the song.

Devotional Discussion 45 minutes

OPTION 1

Discuss, in order, the questions presented in Day 29 thru 35's devotions.

OPTION 2

Discuss which reading from Day 29 thru 35 spiritually challenged you the most? Why was that? What next step is Jesus calling you to take?

Helping Others MEET JESUS 15 minutes

"As you sent me into the world, so I have sent them into the world."
(John 17:18)

Is there anything getting in the way of your **HELPING OTHERS MEET JESUS** plans? How can this obstacle be overcome? What final details need to get covered? Ideally, your effort will be completed before your Session Six meeting.

Prayer   **20 minutes**

Share a prayer request based on what was discussed during this meeting's Devotional Discussion and/or Helping Others Meet Jesus time. What is that next step in your faith life God is calling you to make? What convicted you from God's Word and/or our discussion of His Word? Please also share a way in which the group may support/encourage you regarding what you've shared. Of course other important matters can be prayed about as well. After all have shared, pray for the person on your left (whether aloud or silently). Pray together in popcorn style (as opposed to going in order around a circle).

Coordinating next week's meeting   **5 minutes**

Study Components	Study Component Leader
Worship	
Devotional Discussion	
Helping Others Meet Jesus	
Prayer	
Coordinating	

<u>***Worship Leader***</u>
Leads worship time during meeting.
<u>***Devotional Discussion Leader***</u>
Leads the Bible Study time, encourages application of God's Word to life.
<u>***Helping Others Meet Jesus Leader***</u>
Leads the effort to impact the community to meet Jesus.
<u>***Prayer Leader***</u>
Leads the group prayer time.
<u>***Coordinating Leader***</u>
Coordinates and reminds who will lead the different meeting components.

Read Luke 11:37-54.

"As Jesus was speaking, one of the Pharisees invited him home for a meal. So he went in and took his place at the table. His host was amazed to see that he sat down to eat without first performing the hand-washing ceremony required by Jewish custom. Then the Lord said to him, 'You Pharisees are so careful to clean the outside of the cup and the dish, but inside you are filthy—full of greed and wickedness! Fools! Didn't God make the inside as well as the outside? So clean the inside by giving gifts to the poor, and you will be clean all over.'" (Luke 11:37-41 NLT)

sac · ri · leg · ious - intentional ignorance of a sacred (seemingly holy, traditional) person, place, thing, custom, etc.

Does it seem surprising that Jesus, Son of the Most High God, Holy, God Himself was sacrilegious?

If it wasn't already challenging (impossible without Jesus) for man to live by the 10 Commandments God gave to Moses, Jewish leaders went on to add another 600 plus. Great! (sarcasm implied)

So here comes Jesus in Luke 11 to once again set things right, show people what is truly important in life. Did the required hand-washing ceremony required by Jewish custom account at all for one's salvation? Nope. The custom in and of itself didn't mean a hill of beans. Whereas the custom likely began in reverence to God, ultimately became just another thing to do and check off on one's good-works-to-get-a-gold-star list.

Jesus continued, "What sorrow awaits you Pharisees! For you are careful to tithe even the tiniest income from your herb gardens, but you ignore justice and the love of God. You should tithe, yes, but do not neglect the more important things." (Luke 11:42 NLT)

Jesus is about the important things in life. He is about people, about people knowing His incredible love and grace, about saving people from sin and death. Jesus isn't about handcuffing people to man-made, burden-filled laws, traditions, and customs that truly do no one any good.

How may we introduce people to *Jesus: Sacrilegious* by our words (i.e. communications) and actions? Do some thinking on this. What are things in your life, in the life of your congregation, that may add burden or confusion on those new to the faith or those who are far from God; things which mean nothing for one's salvation?

Read Luke 12:1-12.

Before we get into the account of Jesus in Luke, what do you find to be the benefits of one who warns, namely for the person who would perchance heed the warning? Have you ever warned someone about something? Why did you do so? What was the outcome of your warning?

"Jesus turned first to his disciples and warned them, 'Beware of the yeast of the Pharisees—their hypocrisy.'" (Luke 12:1b NLT)

"Whatever you have said in the dark will be heard in the light, and what you have whispered behind closed doors will be shouted from the housetops for all to hear!" (Luke 12:3 NLT)

"Dear friends, don't be afraid of those who want to kill your body; they cannot do any more to you after that. But I'll tell you whom to fear. Fear God, who has the power to kill you and then throw you into hell. Yes, he's the one to fear." (Luke 12:4-5 NLT)

"...anyone who blasphemes the Holy Spirit will not be forgiven." (Luke 12:10b NLT)

There seems to be some question about the word "warner." A difficult word to find in the dictionary. I read one thread on-line where a person wanted to use the word "warner" (one who warns) but kept getting suggestions from people to instead use "admonisher" or "watchdog." There was also the suggestion of "forewarner". But none of those alternatives convey what I'm trying to get after with ***Jesus: Warner.***

It is just that simple…Jesus was one who warned people on what to watch out for, what to truly fear, and what not to do. He was a warner!

Where in our world do we need Jesus' warnings? Why do we need them? How would Jesus' warnings benefit those in your life who are far from Him?

To whom is God calling you to warn, to introduce *Jesus: Warner* **to? What will be your next step with this?**

Read Luke 12:22-32.

"And don't be concerned about what to eat and what to drink. Don't worry about such things. These things dominate the thoughts of unbelievers all over the world, but your Father already knows your needs. Seek the Kingdom of God above all else, and he will give you everything you need." (Luke 12:29-31 NLT)

Worry. Dread. Anxiety. How many of us are plague by such things? What does it profit us but more of the same?

Lately I've been thinking about how much I need Jesus and what He means to me. In the big scheme of things, what do we need more than Him? He is by our side. He is in our corner. Always and forever.

What does Jesus mean to you? How does He provide for you? How has He provided for you?

As they reached the Red Sea, the Israelites worried as the Egyptians were closing in on them. And then Moses shared these words, "Don't be afraid. Just stand still and watch the Lord rescue you today. The Egyptians you see today will never be seen again. The Lord himself will fight for you. Just stay calm." (Exodus 14:13-14 NLT)

The Lord Jesus does fight for us. He does provide. He fought and provided with His very own life on the cross and came out victorious!

When we are stressed, in need, worried, freaked out, what does Jesus say to us but the same words He shared with Paul, "My grace is all you need." (2 Corinthians 12:9 NLT)

When I think about all of the ways in which Jesus provides for me, I think, "How does a person live their life without Jesus?" I just can't fathom it. And this is why we do what we do. This is why we introduce people to Jesus. This is why we live our lives per His mission to seek and save the lost, those far from knowing Him.

What is your response to all of this?

Read Luke 12:35-48.

[Jesus shared with His disciples,] "Be dressed for service and keep your lamps burning, as though you were waiting for your master to return from the wedding feast. Then you will be ready to open the door and let him in the moment he arrives and knocks. The servants who are ready and waiting for his return will be rewarded. I tell you the truth, he himself will seat them, put on an apron, and serve them as they sit and eat! He may come in the middle of the night or just before dawn. But whenever he comes, he will reward the servants who are ready."

2,000 years before Arnold coined "I'll be back" (sorry, couldn't help myself), Jesus declared His return.

As we meet *Jesus: Returner*, let's look at the good news for us.

First, even after Jesus' death, resurrection and ascension, He never left His people. He shared this promise in Matthew 28:19-20 (NLT), "Therefore, go and make disciples of all the nations, baptizing them in the name of the Father and the Son and the Holy Spirit. Teach these new disciples to obey all the commands I have given you. AND BE SURE OF THIS: I AM WITH YOU ALWAYS, EVEN TO THE END OF THE AGE [my caps]."

Second, He promised that when He went away, He would send the Holy Spirit to be with us. (John 16:7).

Third, He offered these words of encouragement hope and love to His followers, "Don't let your hearts be troubled. Trust in God, and trust also in me. There is more than enough room in my Father's home. If this were not so, would I have told you that I am going to prepare a place for you? When everything is ready, I will come and get you, so that you will always be with me where I am." (John 14:1-3 NLT)

With this good news come questions for our lives.

What does it mean to...
- be dressed for service?
- be ready?
- carry out His instructions?
- be prepared?
- be entrusted with what we've been given?

And considering Jesus' return...
- Where is there the urgency to introduce people to Jesus - the one who saves those who believe in Him from sin and death?

- How does this impact your call from Jesus to "go and make disciples of all the nations, baptizing them in the name of the Father and the Son and the Holy Spirit. Teach these new disciples to obey all the commands I have given you"?

Read Luke 12:49-59.

"Do you think I have come to bring peace to the earth? No, I have come to divide people against each other!" (Luke 12:51 NLT)

Wow, that doesn't sound like Jesus. Not the Jesus we hear generally hear about in our congregations. I could have easily skipped this section of Luke onto an aspect of Jesus that would sound more "favorable" to people….more "nice" Jesus. But if we are to **MEET JESUS**, we need to meet the real Jesus—that includes *Jesus: Divider*.

And go back to read the real Jesus in verses 49-50 (NLT), "I have come to set the world on fire, and I wish it were already burning! I have a terrible baptism of suffering ahead of me, and I am under a heavy burden until it is accomplished." This is about as human and raw as we are going to see. This is 100% Jesus. This is 100% *Jesus: Son of God*. He was sent for a most difficult mission—to give up His life, in the worst way, so that we may be saved. It was serious. Jesus was (is) that serious about us. He loved (loves) us that much.

So how would you introduce *Jesus: Divider* to a friend? What words would you use to explain Jesus' serious, committed, sacrificial love for a world, for a people, steeped in sin and rebellion against Him? How would you explain the good news of *Jesus: Divider*? I won't give you the answers on that. Something to truly wrestle with on your own, with your small group. Take the time to grapple through it.

And so ends our 40 days of **MEET JESUS** devotions. Thanks for sticking through this journey! You may be thinking, "Hey Craig, we haven't even finished Luke. Why did you stop in the middle? There are 12 more chapters to discuss!" Well, therein lies the challenge for you.

In 40 days, we've only begun meeting Jesus and learning all of the nuances and complexities of Him. I invite you to keep reading Luke on your own. Read only the header sections at a time and look closely as to who you find Jesus to be in each section. There is a lot more to say about Jesus than 40 characteristics. Keep going. Keep meeting Him yourself. Keep learning how to introduce who you are meeting to others, especially those who are far from Him. This 40-day journey is over. But your journey in meeting Jesus and introducing others to Him continues! Many blessings!

Worship   **5 minutes**

Whomever is the Worship leader, choose a song that touches you as to who Jesus is. Play the song for the group. Share how you personally **MEET JESUS** through the song.

Devotional Discussion   **45 minutes**
OPTION 1
Discuss, in order, the questions presented in Day 36 thru 40's devotions.

OPTION 2
Discuss which reading from Day 36 thru 40 spiritually challenged you the most? Why was that? What next step is Jesus calling you to take?

Helping Others MEET JESUS   **15 minutes**

> "As you sent me into the world, so I have sent them into the world."
> (John 17:18)

How did your **HELPING OTHERS MEET JESUS** plan go?

What praise reports do you have to share with one another?

How did you see Jesus show up?

What did you learn from the experience?

What would you do differently?

What can your group do to continue helping others in your community to **MEET JESUS** and know His love?

Prayer   **20 minutes**

Share a prayer request based on what was discussed during this meeting's Devotional Discussion and/or Helping Others Meet Jesus time. What is that next step in your faith life God is calling you to make? What convicted you from God's Word and/or our discussion of His Word? Please also share a way in which the group may support/encourage you regarding what you've shared. Of course other important matters can be prayed about as well. After all have shared, pray for the person on your left (whether aloud or silently). Pray together in popcorn style (as opposed to going in order around a circle).

Coordinating next week's meeting   **5 minutes**

Study Components	Study Component Leader
Worship	
Devotional Discussion	
Helping Others Meet Jesus	
Prayer	
Coordinating	

<u>***Worship Leader***</u>
Leads worship time during meeting.
<u>***Devotional Discussion Leader***</u>
Leads the Bible Study time, encourages application of God's Word to life.
<u>***Helping Others Meet Jesus Leader***</u>
Leads the effort to impact the community to meet Jesus.
<u>***Prayer Leader***</u>
Leads the group prayer time.
<u>***Coordinating Leader***</u>
Coordinates and reminds who will lead the different meeting components.

AUTHOR BIO

Craig Mattes, a 2nd career church worker with a certification in Christian outreach, has deep desire for God's Word, witnessing the Word and Spirit do their life-transforming work in the environment of Christian community, and reaching people with the Good News of Jesus. Craig is also a part of FiveTwo (www.fivetwo.com), a network that fuels Christian entrepreneurs who start new to reach new.

You want to start something, anything, that reaches people who don't know Jesus.

We want to help.

StartNew is a two-year start-up incubator that connects you to the camaraderie, courage, and know-how you need so that your start-up will thrive over the long haul.

We assess you.
We teach you.
We coach you.

Go to fivetwo.com/start-training to StartNew today.

fivetwo.com

FiveTwo coaches will walk along side you as you start something new to reach new for Jesus.

We listen.

We help you design action steps that will move you closer to your vision.

We help you discover the Jesus-in-you along the way.

The coaching relationship empowers you to make the difference you know you can make.

let's start something new.

fivetwo.com

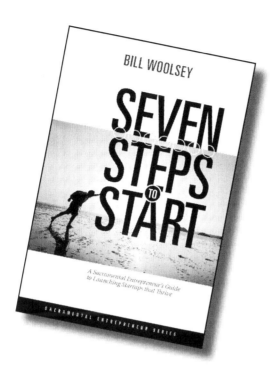

SEVEN STEPS TO START:
A Sacramental Entrepreneur's Guide To Launching Startups That Thrive

In order to reach new people, the church must start new.

Seven Steps to Start is a practical guide for starting new. Whether that be new churches, coffee shops, a missional community, or a new small business, this book will guide you in starting strong.

Sacramental entrepreneurs are those who are both entrepreneurial in their desire to start new and sacramental in their love for God's mysterious work in the sacraments. Sacramental entrepreneurs see themselves and their work as sacramental work as God is mysteriously at work in them for the world.

Order yours today at fivetwo.com/commerce.

fivetwo.com

Made in the USA
Lexington, KY
08 September 2017